WHO'S WHO IN...
50 NAMES YOU NEED TO KNOW!

WORLD RELIGIONS

ANITA GANERI

Published 2008 by
A & C Black Publishers Ltd.
38 Soho Square, London, W1D 3HB
www.acblack.com

Hardback ISBN 978-1-4081-0428-6

Paperback ISBN 978-1-4081-1088-1

This book is produced using paper that is made from wood grown in managed, sustainable forests. It is natural, renewable and recyclable. The logging and manufacturing processes conform to the environmental regulations of the country of origin.

Printed and bound in Malaysia by Times Offset (M) Sdn Bhd.

All the internet addresses given in this book were correct at the time of going to press. The author and publishers regret any inconvenience caused if addresses have changed or sites have ceased to exist, but can accept no responsibility for any such changes.

Acknowledgements
The publishers would like to thank the following for their kind permission to reproduce their photographs:
Cover image: Stephen Coburn Pages: 4 Alison Wright/CORBIS; 5 John Henry Claude Wilson/Robert Harding World Imagery/Corbis; 6 Luca I. Tettoni/CORBIS; 7 Franck Guiziou/Hemis/Corbis; 8 Galen Rowell/CORBIS; 9 Michael Freeman/CORBIS; Urgyen Sangharakshita; 10 Araldo de Luca/CORBIS; Roger Wood/CORBIS; 11 Alinari Archives/CORBIS; 12 Alinari Archives/CORBIS; 13 Alinari Archives/CORBIS; 14 Pascal Deloche/Godong/Corbis; 15 Historical Picture Archive/CORBIS; 16 Christie's Images/CORBIS; 17 Francis G. Mayer/CORBIS; 18 Isu; Dorling Kindersley; 19 Frédéric Soltan/Sygma/Corbis; 20 Luca Tettoni/Corbis; 21 Brooklyn Museum/Corbis; 22 Bettmann/CORBIS; 23 Historical Picture Archive/CORBIS; 24 Hans Georg Roth/Corbis; 25 Michael Freeman/CORBIS; 27 Nabil Mounzer/epa/Corbis; 28 Steve Allen; 29 Ancient Art & Architecture Collection Ltd; 30 Kazuyoshi Nomachi/Corbis; 31 Reuters/CORBIS; 33 Francis G. Mayer/CORBIS; 34 Alinari Archives/Corbis; 35 Summerfield Press/CORBIS; 36 Elio Ciol/CORBIS; 37 National Gallery Collection; By kind permission of the Trustees of the National Gallery, London/CORBIS; 38 Arte & Immagini srl/CORBIS; 39 Bettmann/CORBIS; 40 Time & Life Pictures/Getty Images; Chris Hellier/CORBIS; 41 AFP/Getty Images; AFP/Getty Images; 42 I.F/AAA Collection Ltd; 43 Getty Images; 45 Tibor Bognar/Corbis; Christophe Bolsvieux/Corbis.

Contents

Amitabha

Amitabha is a key figure in a branch of Buddhism known as Pure Land Buddhism. This form of the religion has many followers in China and Japan.

What was said about him

66 There is only One Way, not two or three, (and that way is devotion to Amitabha). 99

(From the "Lotus Sutra")

Did you know?

The *Lotus Sutra* is the most important text of Pure Land Buddhism.

Find out more

This website has more information about Pure Land Buddhism:
www.amtbweb.org/tchet400.htm

Read even more at:
www.religionfacts.com/buddhism/sects/pure_land.htm

Amitabha's story

According to the sacred texts of Buddhism, Amitabha was a king who heard the teachings of the Buddha (⇨p7). Amitabha gave up his throne to become a **monk**. After thousands of years of helping others, Amitabha gained so much merit that he eventually became a buddha.

Timeline

Lotus Sutra written

Early Pure Land monastery founded in China

c. **1st century BC–AD 2nd century**   c. **210**   **402**   c. **476-560**

Lotus Sutra first translated into Chinese

Life of T'an-luan who popularized Pure Land

Place in religion

The followers of Amitabha think that he rules over a heaven-like land called the Pure Land. If people have faith in Amitabha and chant his name, even as few as ten times, they will be reborn in the Pure Land when they die.

Pure Land Buddhism began in India and then spread to China and eventually Japan. Today, it is the most popular form of Buddhism in China, Korea, Japan, Taiwan and Vietnam, where it is practised by millions of people.

Ashoka

Ashoka was an Indian emperor during the 3rd century BC. He was a Hindu by birth but converted (changed) to Buddhism. He sent **missionaries** to spread the **Buddhist** faith far and wide.

About Ashoka

Ashoka came to the throne in 272 BC. He was a brilliant soldier and expanded his empire to cover most of India. One of the few places that did not give way to his rule was Kalinga, on India's east coast. In 260 BC, Ashoka waged war against Kalinga and brought it under his rule.

What he said

❝All men are my children.❞

How did he die?

Ashoka died at the age of 72, after ruling for about 40 years.

Timeline

Born in Pataliputra, India	Battle of Kalinga		Dies in Pataliputra, India			
c. **304 BC**	**272 BC**	**260 BC**	**250 BC**	**232 BC**	**185 BC**	
	Becomes emperor		Introduces Buddhism to Sri Lanka	Empire collapses		

Place in religion

Tens of thousands of people were killed or injured during the war and many more were left homeless. Ashoka was filled with remorse when he realized what he had done. He decided to become a Buddhist. Instead of waging wars, Ashoka wanted to win people over by doing good deeds.

Ashoka carved edicts (laws) on rocks and pillars throughout his empire to announce his beliefs. He also built the Great Stupa at Sanchi, India (shown top right). The Stupa is a symbol of Buddhism. In 250 BC, a group of Ashoka's missionaries introduced Buddhism to Sri Lanka.

Find out more

Find out more information about Ashoka and how he came to be such an important figure in Buddhism: www.religionfacts.com

This site contains the teachings of Ashoka: www.buddhistpilgrimage.info

The "Encyclopedia Britannica" website has more information about Ashoka: www.britannica.com

Avalokiteshvara

Avalokiteshvara is a mythical figure in Buddhism. He is known for his great compassion and care for those who are suffering or in trouble.

About Avalokiteshvara

The name Avalokiteshvara means "the lord who looks in every direction". Images of Avalokiteshvara often show him with one thousand arms. This symbolizes his readiness to help everyone at once. Sometimes he is shown with one thousand eyes to help him see all those who are suffering.

Did you know?

In China, Avalokiteshvara is worshipped as a female called Guan Yin.

Did you know?

In Tibet, the Dalai Lama is thought to be an **incarnation** of Avalokiteshvara.

What was said about him

66 If a person being tossed about in the great sea calls out Avalokiteshvara's name, he will find a shallow place. 99

(From the "Lotus Sutra")

Find out more

Find out more about the life of Avalokiteshvara at:
www.buddhanet.net

The British Museum website features artefacts relating to Avalokiteshvara:
www.britishmuseum.org

This website features a collection of pictures of statues of Avalokiteshvara:
www.collectbritain.co.uk

Place in religion

Having gained **enlightenment**, Avalokiteshvara made a vow to listen to people in need. Buddhists often pray to Avalokiteshvara in times of hardship. They chant the **mantra** "Om, mani padme hum" ("Om, the jewel in the lotus") to call on him to help them lead happier lives. In Tibet, the mantra is carved on rocks and written on pieces of paper. The mantra is also placed inside prayer wheels. Prayer wheels are wooden or metal wheels carved with sacred prayers or mantras. When the wheels are spun, they release the mantras to the world.

The Buddha

The Buddha means "enlightened one". It was the name given to Siddhartha Gautama, whose teachings are followed by Buddhists all over the world.

About the Buddha

Siddhartha Gautama was the son of a wealthy chieftain and had a privileged childhood. At the age of 29, Siddhartha had an experience that changed his life. One day, he took a chariot ride outside the palace and saw many people in great hardship. Then he saw a holy man dressed in rags, who was very calm and serene. Siddhartha decided to give up his wealth and become like this holy man. He spent many years in hardship, living simply and thinking how he could end all the suffering he had seen. Years later, Siddhartha finally gained enlightenment and became the Buddha. He realized that suffering could be ended by people simply being content with what they have.

What he said

66 Better than a thousand useless words is one single word that gives peace. 99

Find out more

Find out more about the Buddha's life and look at some Buddhist artefacts at the British Museum: www.ancient india.co.uk

This site tells you about all aspects of Buddhism, including stories and facts: www.buddhanet.net

The BBC website provides lots of information about Buddhist teachings and festivals: www.bbc.co.uk/schools/religion/buddhism

Timeline

Born in Lumbini, Nepal

Son, Rahula born. Leaves home to live as a monk.

Dies in Kushinagara, India

c. **563 BC**   c. **547 BC**   c. **534 BC**   c. **528 BC**   c. **483 BC**

Marries Princess Yashodhara

Gains enlightenment at Bodh Gaya, India

Place in religion

The Buddha spent the rest of his life as a monk travelling around India, telling people his beliefs. Many of his followers also became monks. When the Buddha died, his teaching spread out of India to other Asian countries and beyond. The religion of Buddhism, based on these teachings, now has more than 350 million followers worldwide.

How did he die?

The Buddha died from food poisoning when he was 80 years old.

Dalai Lama

The Dalai Lama is the leader of the Buddhists of Tibet. The current Dalai Lama lives in India where he and his monks have built up a Tibetan Buddhist community.

What he said

66 My religion is very simple. My religion is kindness. 99

Did you know?

In 1989, the Dalai Lama was awarded the Nobel Peace Prize for his work on human rights.

Place in religion

The title "Dalai Lama" means "ocean of wisdom" and has been given to the head of the Tibetan Buddhists since the 16th century. By the 17th century, the Dalai Lama had become the religious and political leader of Tibet.

Timeline

Born in Tibet on 6 July

Becomes Tibet's head of state

Wins the Nobel Peace Prize

1935   **1940**   **1950**   **1959**   **1989**

Becomes the 14th Dalai Lama

Leaves Tibet after Chinese invade

Find out more

The official website of the Dalai Lama, with the latest news, his teachings, a biography, and lots of photos: www.dalailama.com

Find out more about the Dalai Lama and Tibet at: www.tibet.com

The BBC website includes video and audio clips as well as some background information about the Dalai Lama: www.bbc.co.uk/religion

Tibetan Buddhists think that the Dalai Lama is the **reincarnation** of Avalokiteshvara (⇨p6). When a Dalai Lama dies, a baby is selected according to special signs. The baby is taken to Lhasa, the Tibetan capital, to be educated and trained in his duties.

About the Dalai Lama

The current Dalai Lama, Tenzin Gyatso, was taken to Lhasa at the age of five and made head of state when he was just 16. He is the 14th Dalai Lama. In 1959, the Tibetans rose up against Chinese rule. It became dangerous for the Dalai Lama to stay in Tibet, and he was forced to leave. He went to India, where he lives today with with thousands of devoted Tibetan followers.

Maya

Queen Maya was the mother of Siddhartha Gautama, who later became the Buddha (⇨p7).

Maya's dream

Legend says that Maya dreamed about a white elephant. This was a sign that she would have a baby who would become an exceptional person. She gave birth to her son in a flower garden in India, but died seven days later.

Timeline

Marries King Suddhodana

c. 583 BC

Dreams of white elephant

c. 564 BC

Gives birth to son, Siddhartha Gautama

c. 563 BC

Dies seven days after her son is born

Find out more

Find out more about Queen Maya at: www.khandro.net/ Bud_mother.htm

Venerable Sangharakshita

Venerable Sangharakshita is an English Buddhist monk who established a new form of Buddhism.

About Sangharakshita

Born Denis Lingwood, Sangharakshita took his name after becoming a Buddhist monk in India. He returned to England and taught a new form of Buddhism (the Friends of the Western Buddhist Order) suited to Western society.

Timeline

Born in London, England

1925

Travels to India with the British Army

1944

Becomes a Buddhist monk

1950

1967

Starts the Friends of the Western Buddhist Order

Find out more

This site includes a biography of Venerable Sangharakshita in his own words: www.sangharakshita.org

St. Benedict

St Benedict was a **Christian** leader who composed a set of rules for the monks in his monastery. His text, called *Rule*, is still one of the most important Christian books.

Life of St. Benedict

For many years, Benedict lived in a remote mountain cave. In about 525, he moved to southern Italy and established a monastery. There he wrote his book of rules for monks and nuns. Benedict was made a saint in 1220.

Find out more

Find out more about St. Benedict's life and achievements at:
http://justus.anglican.org/resources/bio/198.html

Timeline

Lives in a cave

Dies in Monte Cassino

c. **480**   c. **500**   c. **525**   c. **550**

Born in Nursia, Italy

Moves to Monte Cassino, Italy, where he composes *Rule*

St. George

George was a Roman soldier who was killed for refusing to give up Christianity. He later became **patron saint** of England. St. George's Day is celebrated on 23 April.

Life of St. George

George was born in Turkey to a wealthy Christian family. He moved to Palestine and joined the Roman army. Later, he gave up life as a soldier and dedicated himself to God. During the **Crusades**, George was chosen to be the patron saint of soldiers.

Find out more

Find out some more information about St. George's life at the BBC website:
www.bbc.co.uk/religion/religions/christianity/saints/george_1.shtml

Timeline

Born in Cappadocia, Turkey

People celebrate St. George's Day for first time

c. **270**   c. **304**   **1222**   c. **1348**

Dies in Palestine on 23 April

Becomes patron saint of England

St. Francis of Assisi

St Francis was the son of a wealthy cloth merchant from Assisi in Italy. He spent most of his life as a monk, teaching people about God. He is the patron saint of animals and of Italy.

Life of St. Francis

Francis was born with the name Giovanni Bernardone, but his father changed it to Francesco. In his twenties, Francis fought in a war between the cities of Assisi and Perugia. He was captured and thrown into prison. He was released when the war ended.

One day, an experience changed Francis's life for ever. He saw an old man dressed in rags and decided to give up the riches left to him by his father. Instead, Francis decided to dedicate himself to God. From then on, he lived as a poor monk, helping the sick and needy.

What he said

"Lord, grant that I might not so much seek to be loved as to love."

How did he die?

St. Francis died in a chapel in his home town of Assisi.

Timeline

Born in Assisi, Italy	Becomes a soldier	Visits holy places in Egypt and Israel	Dies in Assisi	Becomes a saint	Becomes patron saint of Italy
1181 or 1182	1202	1291	1226	1228	1939

Find out more

Find out more about St. Francis of Assisi at: www.newadvent.org/cathen/06221a.htm

Read the Prayer of St. Francis at: www.dlshq.org/saints/francis.htm

Another great site is: http://saints.sqpn.com/saintf01.htm

Place in religion

As a monk, Francis was a popular preacher. People came from far and wide to listen to his teachings, and many became monks themselves. Eventually, they formed the Franciscan Order of monks, named after Francis. Francis and his monks travelled widely, teaching people about God. Francis was known for his kindness and love of animals. After his death, he became the patron saint of animals.

Jesus

Jesus is the main figure in Christianity. Christians believe he is the son of God who was born on Earth to save people from their sins.

What he said

"I am the way, and the truth and the life.**"**

(John 14:6)

How did he die?

Jesus was **crucified** by the Romans at Calvary, outside Jerusalem.

Life of Jesus

Jesus was the son of Joseph, a carpenter, and Mary from Nazareth in Galilee, Palestine. He grew up in Nazareth and may have worked as a carpenter like his father.

Timeline

Born in Bethlehem

Dies in Jerusalem

c. 8-4 BC   **c. AD 27**   **c. AD 30 or 33**   **c. AD 65-140**

Baptized in the River Jordan

Rises from the dead and ascends to heaven

Gospels written

Find out more

Find out more about Christianity at: www.religionfacts.com/christianity/fastfacts.htm

This website presents some facts about the life of Jesus, including the miracles he performed: www.whoisjesus-really.com

Another great site is: www.historyforkids.org/learn/religion/christians/jesus.htm

When Jesus was about 30 years old, he was **baptized** by his cousin, John the Baptist (⇨p13). For the next three years, he travelled from place to place, teaching people about God. In the last week of his life, Jesus arrived in Jerusalem for the **Jewish** Pesach festival. There, he was arrested and sentenced to death. According to the Christian *Bible*, Jesus then came back to life and rose into heaven to be with God. This is known as the Resurrection.

Place in religion

The Resurrection is a key part of Christianity. It gives Christians hope for a future with God. Christians try to follow the example of Jesus in their daily lives and live by his word.

John the Baptist

John the Baptist was a preacher who lived on the banks of the River Jordan in Palestine. He baptized his followers in the water. Jesus (⇨p12) was baptized by John.

Life of John the Baptist

John was the son of a priest called Zachariah and his wife, Elizabeth. Until about AD 27, John lived as a **hermit** in the desert. He dressed in clothes of camel hair and ate locusts and wild honey. After this, John began preaching. Huge crowds flocked to hear him. He told them to confess their sins and then baptized them in the River Jordan. Jesus was baptized by John. King Herod Antipas was afraid of John's popularity. He put John in prison and later had him beheaded.

What he said

❝ Repent, for the kingdom of heaven has come near. ❞

Find out more

Find out more about John the Baptist at: www.catholic.org/saints/saint.php?saint_id=152

This website explains why John the Baptist is so important to the Christian Church: http://saints.sqpn.com/saintj02.htm

Timeline

Born in Judah	Baptized Jesus	Died and possibly buried in Samaria
c. **6-2 BC**	c. **AD 27**	c. **AD 30**

How did he die?

John was beheaded by King Herod Antipas.

Place in religion

Most of what we know about John's life comes from the Christian *Bible*. His mission was to prepare people for the coming of Jesus Christ. He told them that Jesus would be "the Lamb of God" and far greater than he. As St. John, he is remembered on his feast days of 24 June (his birthday) and 29 August (his death). In pictures, he is often shown holding a book or a lamb.

Mary

Mary is an important figure for millions of Christians. They believe that God chose Mary to give birth to his son, Jesus Christ.

What she said

66 My soul magnifies the Lord, my spirit rejoices in God my Saviour; He has looked with favour on his humble servant. 99

How did she die?

Christians think that Mary was taken up into heaven at the end of her life.

Find out more

The BBC website has more information about Mary and her importance in Christianity: www.bbc.co.uk/religion/religions/christianity/history/virginmary_1.shtml

Find out more about Mary's life at: http://christianity.about.com/od/newtestamentpeople/p/marymotherjesus.

Life of Mary

As a young woman, Mary lived in Nazareth in Galilee. She was engaged to Joseph, a local carpenter. The *Bible* tells how, one day, the angel Gabriel appeared to Mary and told her that God had chosen her to be the mother of his son. She gave birth to Jesus in Bethlehem. The family returned to live in Nazareth where Mary spent the next 30 years. She is mentioned a few times in stories about Jesus's life, and she appears by the cross when Jesus is crucified.

Timeline

Gives birth to Jesus
in Bethlehem

c. **8–4 BC**

c. **AD 30 or 33**

Buries her son and
witnesses his resurrection

Place in religion

Mary is an important person for all Christians, but she is particularly honoured by Roman Catholics and Orthodox Christians. Many churches display paintings of Mary on the walls, and worshippers light candles and pray in front of her. Mary is also known as "Our Lady" and "the Blessed Virgin Mary".

Noah

Noah was a figure from the *Bible*. God ordered him to build a huge ship, called an ark, to save his family and Earth's animals from a great flood.

Life of Noah

God decided to destroy the Earth with a huge flood because people had become very wicked. God saw that Noah was good and ordered him to build a wooden ark for himself and his family. God also told Noah to take on board two of each species of animal.

The flood lasted for 150 days and destroyed everything on the Earth. Seven days beforehand, God commanded Noah to enter the ark with his family and the animals. The ark eventually came to rest on Mount Ararat. When the floods went away, Noah built a shrine on Mount Ararat and made offerings to thank God for saving him.

Did you know?

Noah is a prophet ("Nuh") of **Islam**.

What was said about him

66 And Noah went in, and his sons, and his wife, and his sons' wives with him, into the ark, because of the waters of the flood. 99

(Genesis 7:7)

Did you know?

Noah is an important figure in both Christianity and **Judaism**.

Place in religion

God blessed Noah. He told him that if Noah and his family followed God's rules, God would not destroy the Earth again. God put a rainbow in the sky as a reminder. After the flood, Noah became a farmer and planted a vineyard. The *Bible* says that he died 350 years after the flood, at the age of 950. Noah and his family became the ancestors of all the people on Earth.

Find out more

Find out more about Noah at: www.newadvent.org/cathen/11088a.htm

This website includes some facts about Noah and his family: http://en.rodovid.org/wk/Person:32411

St. Paul

St. Paul was an early Christian missionary. He travelled widely, teaching people about Jesus. St. Paul wrote many letters that appear in the New Testament of the Christian *Bible*.

What he said

❝ And now abide faith, hope, charity, these three; but the greatest of these is charity. ❞

(I Corinthians, 13:13)

How did he die?

St. Paul was beheaded on the orders of the Roman emperor Nero.

Find out more

Find out more about St. Paul at the BBC website:
www.bbc.co.uk/religion/religions/christianity/history/paul_1.shtml

The BBC website also features a story about finding St. Paul's tomb at the Vatican:
http://news.bbc.co.uk/1/hi/world/europe/6219656.stm

Life of St Paul

Originally named "Saul", Paul was born in Turkey and brought up as a Jew. As a young man, he **persecuted** the Christians. While travelling to Damascus in Syria, however, he had a vision of Jesus that changed his life. After this, he joined the Christians. He changed his name to Paul and began his new life as a preacher.

Timeline

Travels to Damascus		First missionary journey	
c. **AD 33**	c. **AD 36**	c. **AD 47**	AD 64–67
	Travels to Jerusalem		Dies in Rome

Paul travelled widely around the Mediterranean Sea to spread Christianity. He encouraged Christians to stand by their faith even when they were being persecuted. Paul himself was arrested in Jerusalem and sent for trial. It is believed that he was put to death by the Roman emperor Nero around AD 64–67.

Place in religion

Paul wrote many letters, which form part of the New Testament of the Christian *Bible*. His letters were mostly written to new Christians, offering them advice, guidance, and encouragement. His letters have had a huge influence on Christian thinking.

St. Peter

Peter was a fisherman who became one of the twelve **disciples** of Jesus. He later became the first Christian missionary and the first **bishop** of Rome.

Life of St. Peter

According to the Gospels, Peter was born in Bethsaida in Palestine. His parents called him Simon, but Jesus renamed him Peter when he became a disciple, which means "rock".

Timeline

Jesus dies

AD 30 or 33

c. **AD 30**

Arrives in Rome

Dies in Rome

c. **AD 64 or 67**

What Jesus said about him

❝You are Peter, and on this rock I will build my church. ❞

(Matthew 16:18)

Find out more

Find out more about St. Peter and his relationship to Jesus at:
www.catholic.org/saints/saint.php?saint_id=5358

The BBC website has more information about Peter's life as a disciple:
www.bbc.co.uk/religion/religions/christianity/history/disciples_2.shtml

When Jesus died, Peter became the leader of the Christian community of Jerusalem. He travelled widely to spread the Christian faith. His early journeys are mentioned in the Acts of the Apostles in the New Testament. It is thought that St. Peter was crucified under orders of the Roman Emperor Nero. The great Basilica of St Peter in Rome is thought to mark his burial site.

Place in religion

St. Peter holds a special place in the Roman Catholic Church. Catholics think that Peter was the first **Pope**. Today, the Pope wears a ring showing Peter casting his nets from a fishing boat. Some people celebrate Peter with a feast on 29 June, the day on which he died.

How did he die?

According to the Catholic Church, St. Peter was crucified upside down.

Brahma

As the creator of the universe, Brahma is one of the most important Hindu gods.

About Brahma

Brahma is usually pictured with four heads from which came the four *Vedas* (ancient Hindu sacred texts). In his four arms, Brahma holds a spoon used in worship, a pot of holy water, a string of prayer beads, and the *Vedas*. Brahma's companion is Saraswati, goddess of knowledge.

Find out more

Find out more about Brahma at:
www.sanatansociety.org/
hindu_gods_and_goddesses/
brahma.htm

Brahma is the first of three important Hindu gods. The other two gods are Shiva and Vishnu. There are thousands of temples (called mandirs) dedicated to Vishnu and Shiva. Very few Hindus worship Brahma and there are only two mandirs dedicated to him, in India.

Brahman

Brahman is the supreme spirit of Hinduism. The Om symbol (left) stands for Brahman and creation. The different Hindu gods represent Brahman's many different qualities and forms.

About Brahman

Find out more

Find out more about Brahman at the BBC website:
www.bbc.co.uk/religion/
religions/hinduism/beliefs/
intro_1.shtml

Brahman is everywhere but cannot be seen. Hindus think that Brahman lives outside the material world in which we live. The material world does not last and changes constantly. Hindus believe Brahman will live for ever.

To teach his son about Brahman, a wise man put some salt in water. The salt dissolved in the water. The wise man told his son that the salt was like Brahman, invisible but everywhere in India.

Durga

Durga is a beautiful, war-like goddess. She is worshipped across India, especially in the eastern state of Bengal.

About Durga

According to Hindu sacred texts, Durga was created to fight a terrible buffalo-demon called Mahish. Thinking himself to be **invincible**, Mahish spread terror and misery across the world. He was eventually killed by Durga.

Durga is pictured with ten arms for carrying her various weapons. The weapons were given to her by the gods. Durga rides on a lion or tiger. She blows a conch shell to call her warriors to battle.

Did you know?

In **Sanskrit**, the name *Durga* means "invincible".

What was said about her

" O Durga! You have destroyed the troublesome demons and brought peace to the whole world. What greater deeds can there possibly be? "

(From the "Devi Mahatmya")

Find out more

Find out more about Durga at: www.sanatansociety.org/ hindu_gods_and_goddesses/durga.htm

This site looks at the different forms of Durga and what she represents: http://hinduism.about.com/od/ hindugoddesses/a/durga.htm

Place in religion

Many temples are dedicated to Durga throughout India. Each year, in October or November, Hindus remember her great victory over the Mahish at a great festival called the Durga Puja. The festival lasts for nine days. During it, Hindus visit the temple to welcome Durga to Earth. They unveil a special image of the goddess. On the last day, they carry Durga's image around their neighbourhood and then throw it into a river or lake.

Did you know?

The Durga Puja is the biggest religious festival in Bengal.

Ganesh

Ganesh is a Hindu god who has the head of an elephant. Hindus worship him before starting new tasks. They think he can remove all obstacles.

About Ganesh

Several stories explain how Ganesh got his elephant head. One tells the story of Parvati, wife of Shiva. Parvati made a baby boy called Ganesh out of clay to keep her company while Shiva was away. When Shiva returned three years later, he cut off Ganesh's head in a temper. Parvati sent Shiva to find a new head for her baby boy. The first creature he found was an elephant.

Did you know?

Ganesh used one of his tusks to write the Hindu sacred text, *Mahabharata*.

Did you know?

Pictures of Ganesh are often painted above doors and on walls to bring good luck.

Prayer to Ganesh

66 Oh, Lord Ganesh, with a curved trunk and large body. Shining with the light of a million suns. Take away any obstacles. 99

Find out more

Find out more about Ganesh at: www.crystalinks.com/ganesh.html

The BBC website has more information about Ganesh and his importance to Hindus: www.bbc.co.uk/religion/religions/ hinduism/holydays/ganesh.shtml

Another great site about Ganesh is: www.sanatansociety.org/ hindu_gods_and_goddesses/ganesha.htm

Place in religion

Ganesh is the Hindu god of wisdom and good fortune. Hindus ask for his blessing before beginning any new task, such as getting married, moving house, or setting off on a long journey. They celebrate Ganesh's birthday at the festival of Ganesh Chaturthi in August or September. In Mumbai, India, people make huge clay figures of Ganesh. They parade the figures around Mumbai before throwing them into the sea.

Krishna

Krishna is one of the most popular Hindu gods. The young god grew up in a cowherd's village but later became a warrior and hero.

About Krishna

Hindus think that Krishna was an earthly incarnation (**avatar**) of the god Vishnu (⇨p25). Legend says that Krishna was the eighth child of a princess, Devaki, and her husband, Vasudeva. Devaki's brother was the wicked King Kamsa who wanted to kill Krishna. Vasudeva smuggled Krishna out of the palace and took him to the village of Gokul, where he was brought up by a cowherd and his wife. Krishna later returned to the palace to kill King Kamsa.

Did you know?

In pictures, Krishna is usually shown with blue or black skin, playing a flute.

What he said

66 Set your heart on doing your duty, but never on its reward. Do not work for a reward, but never stop doing your duty. 99

Did you know?

Krishna is often worshipped with his companion, Radha.

Place in religion

Krishna is a popular god and widely worshipped. Hindus devote themselves to Krishna and show their love for him through songs. Krishna is also the hero of the sacred Hindu text called the *Bhagavad Gita*. The words of the book are written as if they have been spoken by Krishna. In the book, Krishna tells Prince Arjuna that it is important to do his duty without needing a reward.

Find out more

Find out about Krishna's life and his place in the Hindu faith:
www.sanatansociety.org/hindu_gods_and_goddesses/krishna.htm

This site is all about Janamashtami, the festival that celebrates the birth of Krishna:
www.bbc.co.uk/religion/religions/hinduism/holydays/janamashtami.shtml

The official Hare Krishna website:
www.harekrishna.com

Lakshmi

Lakshmi is the Hindu goddess of wealth and beauty. She is also companion to the god Vishnu (⇨p25). She is worshipped during the Diwali festival.

About Lakshmi

One story about Lakshmi is called "The Churning of the Sea of Milk". Once, Lakshmi was companion of the god Indra. She helped him to protect the world against demons. One day, Indra upset Lakshmi, so she left the world of the gods and went into a sea of milk. The world grew dark without Lakshmi, and the gods lost their powers. Vishnu told the gods to stir the sea of milk to bring Lakshmi back. After many years of stirring, Lakshmi rose to the surface on a lotus flower. The gods became powerful again and defeated the demons.

Did you know?

Lakshmi is usually shown as a beautiful woman standing on a lotus flower.

Did you know?

Lakshmi is sometimes shown riding an owl

What they said about her

" Glory to you, O goddess Lakshmi. Shiva, Vishnu and Brahma meditate on you every day and every night. "

(Prayer to Lakshmi)

Find out more

Find out more about Lakshmi at: www.koausa.org/Gods/God6.html

Another great site is: www.bbc.co.uk/religion/religions/hinduism/deities/lakshmi.shtml

Place in religion

Hindus worship Lakshmi during the festival of Diwali in October or November. People put lamps outside their homes, hoping to welcome Lakshmi inside. Lakshmi will then bless them with luck and good fortune.

Rama

Rama was born on the Earth as a prince. He is believed to be a form of the god Vishnu (⇨p25). His story is told in the sacred Hindu text, *Ramayana*.

About Rama

Rama was the son and heir of King Dasharatha, who ruled Ayodhya in India. Rama's stepmother had her own son. She wanted him to be king of Ayodhya instead of Rama. Rama's stepmother banished Rama and his family to the forest. One day, when Rama was out hunting, a ten-headed demon-king called Ravana kidnapped his wife. Rama set out to rescue her. With the help of Hanuman, son of the god of the wind, and an army of monkeys and bears, Rama killed Ravana. He then returned to the kingdom of Ayodhya to be crowned king.

Did you know?

It is said that Rama brought goodness and order to the world by killing Ravana.

Find out more

This website tells the story of Rama as told in the Hindu sacred text, the "Ramayana": www.sanatansociety.org/indian_epics_and_stories/ramayana_ram.htm

Find out more about the festival of Dassehra: http://web1.mtnl.net.in/~kal1/dassehra.htm

Another great site, with pictures: www.koausa.org/Gods/God4.html

What they said about him

66 Whoever reads the Ramayana daily, all their sins will be washed away. 99

(The "Ramayana")

Place in religion

In September, Hindus celebrate Rama's victory over Ravana at the festival of Dassehra. Travelling actors perform a play, called the *Rama Lila,* based on the story. He is celebrated again at the festival of Diwali. Then Hindus light tiny lamps, called divas, to guide Rama home.

Did you know?

For Hindus, Rama is a symbol of the ideal way of life. He is the ideal son, husband, and king.

Shiva

Shiva is one of the three most important Hindu gods. He is a powerful god, who can destroy or change things.

About Shiva

Shiva is usually shown dressed in animal skins. He holds a three-pronged spear. (The three prongs stand for Brahma, Vishnu, and Shiva.) Shiva's hair is long and matted, and he wears a necklace of poisonous snakes. The third eye in the middle of his forehead represents his wisdom and insight. Shiva is often shown with a blue face and throat. Legend says that his throat turned blue when he drank poison from the sea of milk (⇨p22). Shiva is usually shown dancing. This provides the energy to keep the universe going. If Shiva stops dancing, it is said the universe will end.

What he said

66 Lord, when deadly poison came from the ocean, out of compassion, you drank the poison and saved the world. Your throat became blue and you are known as Nilakantha. 99

(Prayer to Shiva from the "Vedas")

Find out more

Find out about the importance of Shiva in Hinduism at:
www.sanatansociety.org/
hindu_gods_and_goddesses/shiva.htm

See images of Shiva at:
www.bbc.co.uk/religion/religions/
hinduism/deities/shiva.shtml

Another great site about Shiva is:
www.koausa.org/Gods/God9.html

Place in religion

Hindus see Shiva as both good and evil. They think that Shiva destroys the universe to make way for a better one. All over India, mandirs are dedicated to Shiva. Outside each one stands a statue of Nandi, the giant bull on which Shiva rides.

Vishnu

Vishnu is the protector of the universe. He is one of the three most important Hindu gods.

About Vishnu

Vishnu is usually shown standing on a lotus flower or lying on the coils of a huge snake, called Sesa. In his four hands, he holds a conch shell. When he blows the shell, it makes the sound "Om". This is the sound of creation.

Did you know?

Vishnu's companion is the goddess, Lakshmi.

What is said about him

66 O leader of gods! O joy of people!
The one who is kind to seekers of knowledge!
O destroyer of demons! O beloved of Lakshmi!
Be victorious! 99

(From the "Ramcharitmanas" by Tulsidas)

Did you know?

Vishnu rides on a giant eagle, called Garuda – the king of the birds.

Place in religion

Hindus think that Vishnu returns to Earth in different forms. The ten forms of Vishnu are:

1 Matsya, the fish
2 Kurma, the turtle
3 Varaha, the boar
4 Narasimha, the man-lion
5 Vamana, the wise dwarf
6 Parasurama, the warrior
7 Rama (⇨p23)
8 Krishna (⇨p21)
9 The Buddha (⇨p7)
10 Kalki, a rider on a white horse

Find out more

This website includes lots of images showing the forms of Vishnu:
www.sanatansociety.org/
hindu_gods_and_goddesses/vishnu.htm

This website tells the story of how the gods came to live forever:
www.bbc.co.uk/religion/religions/
hinduism/deities/vishnu.shtml

Find out about Matsya at:
http://timepiece.shubhkaamna.com/
vishnu.htm

Abu Bakr

Abu Bakr was the closest companion of the Prophet Muhammad. He joined Muhammad on his journey to Madinah in AD 622.

What he said

66 Without knowledge action is useless, and knowledge without action is futile. 99

How did he die?

Abu Bakr died of food poisoning or a fever. He was buried beside Muhammad.

Find out more

This website includes a list of quotes by Abu Bakr about how to live according to Islam:
www.brainyquote.com/quotes/authors/a/abu_bakr.html

This website tells the story of Abu Bakr and how he helped to spread Islam:
http://anwary-islam.com/companion/abu_bakr_siddiq.htm

Life of Abu Bakr

Abu Bakr was born into a wealthy family in Makkah, the **Muslim** holy city. As an adult, he became good friends with his neighbour, Muhammad. In AD 610, he became the first person outside Muhammad's family to become a Muslim. He earned the title "al-Siddiq" ("the truthful one") for his loyalty. When the Muslims were forced to leave Makkah, he joined Muhammad on the hijra ("flight") to Madinah. On the flight, they hid in the caves shown top left. In Madinah, Muhammad married Abu Bakr's daughter, Aisha.

Timeline

Born in Makkah		Becomes a Muslim		Muhammad dies; becomes Caliph	
c. 570	591	610	622	632	634
	Becomes a cloth trader		Travels to Madinah		Dies in Madinah

Place in religion

When Muhammad died in AD 632, Abu Bakr was chosen as the first Caliph (leader) of the Muslims. In his short time as leader, he stopped a rebellion against his rule. He also began an Islamic empire by conquering Iran, Iraq, and the Middle East. Abu Bakr collected Muhammad's beliefs into the *Qur'an*, the holy book of Islam.

Ali

Ali ibn Abi Talib was the cousin and son-in-law of Prophet Muhammad. He was chosen to be the fourth Caliph (leader) in AD 656.

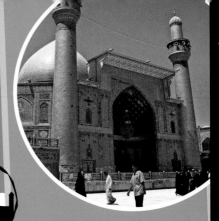

Life of Ali

Ali became a Muslim at an early age. He stood by Muhammad loyally when the Muslims were almost driven out of Makkah. He followed Muhammad to Madinah. Later, he married Muhammad's daughter, Fatimah. Ali fought bravely in many of the early Islamic wars.

What he said

❝ A virtuous person is better than virtue, and a vicious person is worse than vice. **❞**

Timeline

Born in Makkah		Travels to Madinah		Chosen as fourth Caliph (leader)		
c. 599 or 600	610	622	632	656	661	
	Becomes a Muslim		Muhammad dies		Dies in Kufa, Iraq	

Ali worked as an advisor during the reigns of the first three Caliphs (leaders). When Uthman, the third Caliph, was killed, Ali was chosen to lead the Muslims. The first **civil war** in Islamic history took place during Ali's reign. Many Muslims also rose against him, including Muhammad's wife, Aisha, and the governor of Syria.

Place in religion

All Muslims respect Ali for his knowledge and devotion to Islam. But they have different views about his role as Caliph. Some Muslims, called Sunni Muslims, think that Abu Bakr (⇨p26) was Muhammad's rightful successor. Others, called Shi'a Muslims, think that Ali should have succeeded Muhammad, not Abu Bakr.

Find out more

Find out more about Ali at:
http://anwary-islam.com/companion/ali-bin-%20abi-%20talib.htm

Read more about the life of Ali at:
www.kinghussein.gov.jo/hash_ali.html

Another great site about Ali:
http://answering-islam.org/Index/A/ali.html

This site answers your questions about the "Qur'an":
http://answering-islam.org/Quran/index.html

How did he die?

Ali was killed with a poison-coated sword. He was buried in a mosque in Iran (shown above).

Allah

Allah is the **Arabic** word for "God" (shown left). Muslims obey the will of Allah and follow Allah's guidance.

About Allah

Muslims think that Allah is the one true God who created the world and rules over everything. Allah is eternal (lives for ever). Allah has no shape or form and cannot be seen or heard. Allah is just and merciful, and he rewards and punishes people fairly. Muslims believe that they can approach Allah by praying and quoting the *Qur'an*.

Find out more

Find out more about Allah at:
www.allah.org

The Shahadah is a prayer that sums up the belief of all Muslims. It says: "There is no god but Allah; Muhammad is Allah's messenger".

Hagar

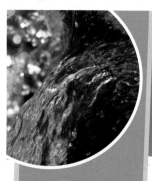

The Egyptian princess Hagar became the second wife of the Prophet Ibrahim (⇨p29) and the mother of their son, Ishma'il (⇨p30).

About Hagar

According to Islamic tradition, Allah ordered Ibrahim to leave Hagar and Ishma'il in the desert at Makkah. Allah wanted to test Ibrahim's obedience. Ibrahim did as Allah wished. After a few days in the desert, Hagar and Ishma'il ran out of water. Hagar ran to find water but collapsed. When Ishma'il tapped the ground with his foot, a spring of water gushed up. Allah had provided for them.

Find out more

Find out more about Hagar at:
http://answering-islam.org/
Index/H/hagar.html

The spring of water became known as the Well of Zam Zam (above left). Muslims visit the well on the **Hajj**.

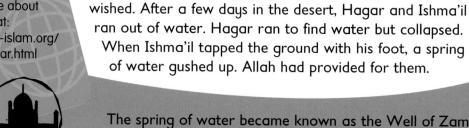

Ibrahim

Ibrahim is a Prophet of Islam. He is famous for his obedience to Allah. As Abraham (⇨p33), Ibrahim is important in other world religions.

Life of Ibrahim

The story of Ibrahim's early life is told in the *Qur'an*. The holy book tells the story of how Allah asked Ibrahim to sacrifice (kill) his son, Ishma'il, as a test of his devotion. Ibrahim got ready to sacrifice his son, but Allah stopped him. Ibrahim had passed the test, and Allah sent him a sheep to sacrifice instead.

Did you know?

Ibrahim is buried in a tomb in the Cave of the Patriarchs in Hebron, Palestine (shown above).

What he said

66 Praise be to Allah, who has given me in old age Ishma'il and Ishaq. Most surely my Lord is the hearer of my prayers. 99

("Qur'an" 14:39)

Did you know?

Muslims must turn to face the **Ka'bah** in Makkah when they pray.

Place in religion

Muslims think that Ibrahim was a messenger sent by Allah to teach Muslims how to live according to Allah's wishes. During the Hajj (a holy journey to Makkah that takes place each year), Muslims remember Ibrahim and Ishma'il and visit various sites around Makkah. Ibrahim and Ishma'il rebuilt the Ka'bah in Makkah, the holiest place in the Muslim world. At the end of the Hajj, Muslims celebrate the festival of Id-ul-Adha by sacrificing a sheep or goat.

Find out more

Find out about Ibrahim's life and how he became a Muslim at: www.islamicity.com/Mosque/ibrahim.htm

Read an account of Ibrahim, Ishma'il, and Hagar's trip to the Valley of Makkaha: www.rasoulallah.net/subject_en.asp?hit=1&parent_id=527&sub_id=5561

This site takes a look at Ibrahim's role in different religions: http://i-cias.com/e.o/abraham.htm

Ishma'il

Ishma'il is a Prophet of Islam. He helped his father, Ibrahim (⊏>p9), rebuild the Ka'bah in Makkah (left).

About Ishma'il

Ishma'il is one of the Prophets of Islam in the *Qur'an*. He is also believed to be the ancestor of the Arab people. Muslim tradition tells the story of how Ishma'il and his mother were left in the desert by Ibrahim (⊏>p29). According to the *Qur'an*, Ibrahim (Ishma'il's father) was later asked to sacrifice his son to show his devotion to Allah.

The *Qur'an* does not say that Isma'il was the child left in the desert in the story above. However, Muslims believe that it was him. The family was later reunited and Ishma'il and his father rebuilt the Ka'bah.

Find out more

Read the story of the Prophet Ishma'il at:
www.anwary-islam.com/
prophet-story/ishmael.htm

Jibril

Jibril is the angel who brought Allah's wishes to each of the Prophets of Islam.

About Jibril

Muslims think that angels are Allah's messengers. Jibril helped the Prophet Muhammad (⊏>p32) to write the words of the *Qur'an*. He first showed the words to Muhammad in the cave on Mount Hira, near Makkah (left). He also guided Muhammad on his night journey up into heaven. There Muhammad met the Prophets who had come before him.

Find out more

Learn more about the angels of Islam at:
www.geocities.com/khola_mon/
myth/Angels.html

Khadijah

Khadijah was the first wife of the Prophet Muhammad (⇨p32). She was the first person to convert to Islam.

Life of Khadijah

Khadijah came from a wealthy family. When her father died, Khadijah managed the family business. Khadijah was successful and became very wealthy. Muhammad went to work for her, and she sent him on several journeys selling and buying goods. They married and were very happy together. They had four daughters and two sons, both of whom died.

What Muhammad said about her

66 She accepted Islam when people rejected me. 99

Timeline

Born in Makkah		Dies in Makkah
C. **555**	C. **605**	C. **619 or 623**
	Marries Muhammad	

How did she die?

Khadijah died in AD 619 or 623. She was buried in Makkah.

Place in religion

When Allah told Muhammad to call people to worship him, Khadijah was the first person to obey his command. She became the first person to convert to Islam. In the following years, she stood by Muhammad as the powerful leaders of Makkah tried to destroy the Muslims and drive them out of their city.

Find out more

Find out more about Khadijah at: www.islamfortoday.com/khadijah.htm

This website includes information about the wives of Muhammad: www.angelfire.com/on/ummiby1/wives1.html

Another great site: www.islamproject.org/muhammad/muhammad_05_BioSketchofMuhammad.htm

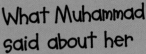

Muhammad

Muhammad was the greatest of the Prophets chosen by Allah (⇨p28).

Life of Muhammad

Orphaned at a young age, Muhammad was brought up by his grandfather and uncle. He later worked as a merchant in Makkah and married a rich widow, Khadijah (⇨p31).

What he said

66 They will enter Paradise who have a true, pure and merciful heart. **99**

How did he die?

Muhammad died in Madinah. The Mosque of the Prophet stands above his tomb.

Timeline

First revelation of the *Qur'an*

Born in Makkah

Dies in Madinah

570   **595**   **610**   **622**   **632**

Marries Khadijah

Hijrah (migration) to Madinah

Find out more

This website shows the place of Islam in the modern world:
http://muhammad.net/j/index.php

Timeline of the important events of Muhammad's life:
www.ucalgary.ca/~elsegal/I_Transp/103_Life_of_Muhammad.html

Find out more about Muhammad and his place in Islam:
http://atschool.eduweb.co.uk/carolrb/Islam/muhammad.html

One night, while Muhammad was **meditating** in a cave on Mount Hira, he met the angel Jibril (⇨p30). After this, Muhammad began to teach people about Islam.

Place in religion

Muslims think that Islam has always existed but that Muhammad "completed" the teaching of Islam to the world. They do not worship Muhammad as a god but honour him as a special human being. To show their respect, they always say the words "Peace be upon him" after his name. In their daily lives, Muslims try to follow the example of how Muhammad lived and what he said. The image top left shows the name Muhammad written in Arabic.

Abraham

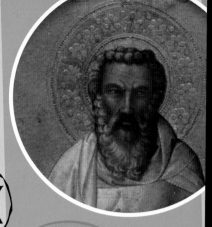

Abraham is the founding father of the Jewish people. He lived about 4,000 years ago in the Middle East.

Life of Abraham

According to the **Hebrew** *Bible*, Abraham was born in the city of Ur in Mesopotamia (modern-day Iraq) around 1800 BC. At that time, people believed in many gods but Abraham worshipped one God. Abraham's God told him to go to Canaan (now Israel), where he would become the father of a great people. Abraham obeyed his new God.

Did you know?

Abraham was buried next to Sarah, his wife, in the Cave of the Patriarchs near Hebron.

What the Bible says

66 Now the Lord said to Abraham, Leave your country and your home, and your father's house. Go to the country that I will show to you. And I will make you a great nation. 99

(Genesis 12:1–2)

Find out more

Find out more about Abraham at: www.jewishvirtuallibrary.org/jsource/biography/abraham.html

The BBC website has more information about Abraham in the context of other world religions: www.bbc.co.uk/religion/religions/judaism/history/abraham_1.shtml

Place in religion

Abraham placed his trust in God and obeyed him, even though it meant leaving his home for the unknown. God continued to test Abraham. He asked Abraham to sacrifice his own son, Isaac. Abraham was ready to obey, but God stopped him at the last moment.

Abraham is a great figure in three world religions – Judaism, Christianity, and Islam (⇨p29 Ibrahim). These are sometimes called the "Abrahamic religions".

Did you know?

Abraham had two sons – Isaac with his wife, Sarah, and Ishma'il with his wife, Hagar.

David

David was the second king of Israel after King Saul. He was a skilled poet and he may have written many of the **Psalms**.

What he said

66 The Lord is my shepherd; I shall not want. He leads me in the paths of righteousness for His name's sake. 99

(From Psalm 23)

How did he die?

According to Jewish texts, David was born and died on the Jewish festival of Shavuot.

Life of David

The story of David's life is told in the books of Samuel and Chronicles in the Hebrew *Bible*. David was born about 3,000 years ago and grew up in Bethlehem. After David killed the giant, Goliath, Saul appointed him to command his army. Saul gave him his daughter, Michal, to marry. After Saul's death, David became king of Judah and then of all Israel. He made his capital in Jerusalem. In the later years of his reign, two of David's sons rebelled against him. After David died, his son Samuel became king.

Timeline

Born in Bethlehem

c. **1037 BC**

c. **1000 BC**

Becomes king of Israel

c. **967 BC**

Dies in Jerusalem

Find out more

Read an account of David's life at: www.jewishvirtuallibrary.org/jsource/ biography/David.html

Find out more about David and Goliath at: www.jesus-is-lord.com/goliath.htm

Place in religion

Jews think that God chose David and his descendants to rule the Jewish people for ever. They honour him as a great scholar and poet and credit him as the author of many of the Psalms. David is also important in other world religions. In Islam, he is known as the Prophet Dawud.

Esther

The story of Esther is told in the Book of Esther in the Hebrew *Bible*. Esther was a young Jewish woman who married a Persian king and saved the lives of the Jewish people.

Life of Esther

Esther was the wife of the Persian king Xerxes I. The king had a chief minister, called Haman, who wanted everyone to bow when they saw him. Esther's cousin, Mordecai, refused. Haman was furious and told the king to kill all the Jews in Persia. Mordecai visited Esther and asked for her help. Esther invited the king to a feast. She told him that she was Jewish and that Haman wanted to kill her people. The king was furious and ordered Haman to be killed instead. Mordecai was appointed chief minister.

What she said

66 If I have found favour in your sight, O king... let my life be given me at my petition, and my people at my request. 99

(Esther 7:3)

Did you know?

One of the messages of Purim is that God always makes sure that good wins in the end.

Timeline

Reign of Xerxes I begins		Esther saves Jewish people from death		
486 BC	c. **480 BC**	c. **470 BC**	**465 BC**	
	Esther marries Xerxes I		Xerxes I dies	

Find out more

Find out more about Esther at this "Bible" study website: www.keyway.ca/htm2002/estherb.htm

Find out about the festival of Purim at: www.bbc.co.uk/religion/religions/judaism/holydays/purim_1.shtml

Place in religion

Every year, in February or March, Jews remember Esther's courage at the festival of Purim. The story is read out at a service in the **synagogue**. Whenever Haman is mentioned, children in the congregation boo, hiss, stamp their feet, and shake rattles, called greggors, to drown out the sound of his name.

Isaac

Isaac was the son of Abraham (⇨p33) and the second father (patriarch) of the Jewish people.

Life of Isaac

The story of Isaac is told in the Book of Genesis in the Hebrew *Bible*. His name comes from a Hebrew word meaning "laughter". Jewish tradition says that the sun shone particularly brightly on the day when Isaac was born. Some years later, God tested Abraham's faith by asking him to sacrifice Isaac. Isaac calmly agreed that his father must follow God's wishes. Abraham passed the test, so God stopped the sacrifice before it was too late.

Did you know?

Isaac married Rebekah, and they had twin sons, Esau and Jacob.

How did he die?

Isaac is said to have died at Hebron, at the age of 180 years old.

What is said about him

66 And Abraham called the name of his son that was born to him, whom Sarah bore, Isaac. 99

(Genesis 21:3)

Find out more

Find out more about Isaac at:
www.rationalchristianity.net/abe_isaac.html

This website tells the story of Abraham and Isaac:
www.usbible.com/Sacrifice/AbrahamIsaac.htm

Find out more about the origins of Judaism at:
www.jewfaq.org/origins.htm

Place in religion

Isaac became the father of the Jewish people after his father Abraham died. In Jewish tradition, Isaac "went out to meditate at eventide". Jews say prayers in the synagogue (Jewish temple) in the afternoon in memory of Isaac. Isaac is also important in other world religions. In Islam, he is known as the Prophet Ishaq.

Jacob

Jacob was the son of Isaac (⇨p36) and the third father (patriarch) of the Jewish people.

Life of Jacob

When Isaac was 40 years old, he married Rebekah. They had twin sons, Esau and Jacob. Esau was born first, so he was set to inherit his father's wealth. Jealous of his brother, Jacob tricked Esau into giving his birthright away. Then Jacob tricked his father into giving him his blessing, too. Esau wanted to kill Jacob, so Rebekah sent Jacob to stay with his uncle in Haran. On the way, Jacob dreamed of a ladder reaching from earth to heaven. God appeared above the ladder and promised to give the land of Canaan to Jacob's descendants.

What is said about him

66 And [Jacob] dreamed, and saw a ladder set up on the earth, and the top it reached to heaven: and behold the angels of God ascending and descending on it. 99

(Genesis 28:12)

Place in religion

In Haran, Jacob married two wives, Leah and Rachel. Jacob and his wives had twelve sons and one daughter. His twelve sons were Reuben, Simeon, Levi, Judah, Issachar, Zebulun, Joseph, Benjamin, Dan, Naphtali, Gad and Asher. They were the ancestors of the twelve tribes of Israel (the traditional division of the Jewish people).

Did you know?

Jacob eventually went to live in Egypt where his favourite son, Joseph, had settled.

Find out more

Find out more about Jacob's life at: www.chabad.org/library/article_cdo/aid/246619/jewish/Jacob-Receives-Isaacs-Blessing.htm

Find out more about Jacob at this "Bible" study website: www.biblestudyguide.org/children-biblestories/gen_27-isaac-jacob.htm

Another great site about Jacob and his place in Jewish history: www.jewishencyclopedia.com/view.jsp?artid=19&letter=J&search=jacob

How did he die?

Tradition says that Jacob died in Egypt at the age of 147 years old.

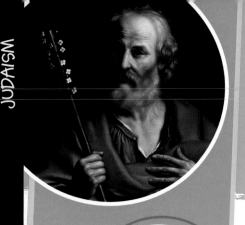

Joseph

Joseph was the favourite son of Jacob (➪p35). His brothers were jealous, so they got rid of him. Joseph ended up in Egypt, where he became a powerful governor to the **Pharaoh**.

Life of Joseph

The story of Joseph is told in the Book of Genesis in the Hebrew *Bible*. Joseph was the son of Jacob and Rachel. Jacob loved Joseph very much and gave him many gifts, including a "coat of many colours". Joseph's brothers were jealous. They threw Joseph into a pit where he was found by passing merchants. The merchants sold Joseph as a slave in Egypt. There, Joseph's worked out the meaning of the Pharaoh's dreams. His skill earned him the job of governor of Egypt. He was responsible for giving out grain during a famine. Among the people who came to him were his brothers, who had come to buy corn. Joseph forgave his brothers. Eventually, the whole family, including Jacob, settled in Egypt.

Did you know?

In the *Qur'an*, Joseph's brothers throw him into a well and tell Jacob that a wolf had eaten him.

How did he die?

Tradition says that Joseph lived to the age of 110 and was buried in Nablus, Palestine.

Find out more

Find out more about the story of Joseph and his brothers at:
www.chabad.org/library/article_cdo/aid/246624/jewish/Joseph-and-His-Brothers.htm

This website tells the story of Joseph and his coat of many colours:
www.keyway.ca/htm2002/coatcol.htm

Another great site about Joseph:
www.topmarks.co.uk/judaism/joseph/joseph.htm

What he said

66 And Joseph said to his brothers, I am Joseph; does my father still live? And his brothers could not answer him; for they were troubled by his presence. 99

(Genesis 45:3)

Place in religion

Joseph has a very important place in Jewish religious teaching. He is seen as an example of a respectful son and loyal brother. Joseph is also important in other world religions. In Islam, he appears as the Prophet Yusuf.

Moses

Moses led the Jews out of slavery in Egypt. He received God's revelation of the *Torah*, including the Ten Commandments.

Life of Moses

The story of Moses is told in to the Book of Exodus in the Hebrew *Bible*. Moses was born in Egypt. At the time, Jews in Egypt were treated like slaves. The Pharaoh gave an order than every Jewish baby boy was to be killed. So Moses's mother, Jochebed, put her baby in a basket and hid him in the reeds by the River Nile. The Pharaoh's daughter found Moses and brought him up as her own son.

Did you know?

In Islam, Moses is known as the Prophet Musa.

What he said

66 And she called his name Moses: and she said, Because I drew him out of the water. 99

(Exodus 2:14)

How did he die?

According to the Bible, Moses died on Mount Nebo in Moab at the age of 120.

God called on Moses to lead the Jews out of Egypt. Moses led them across the Red Sea and through the desert. On Mount Sinai, he received the *Torah* from God. Before his death, he appointed Joshua to lead the Jews safely to Canaan.

Place in religion

The *Torah* is the most important of the Jewish scriptures. Moses also taught the Jews the Ten Commandments – ten rules given by God. These events are celebrated during the **pilgrim** festivals of Sukkot, Pesach, and Shavuot.

Find out more

Find out more about Moses at: www.topmarks.co.uk/judaism/moses/index.htm

This website tells the story of Moses as a baby: www.dltk-bible.com/exodus/story_of_baby_moses_cv.htm

Ruth

Ruth was a non-Jewish widow, who was the great-grandmother of King David (⇨p34).

About Ruth

The story of Ruth is told in the Book of Ruth in the Hebrew *Bible*. When her first husband died, Ruth left her own country and made her home in Bethlehem with her Jewish mother-in-law, Naomi. Eventually, she remarried a wealthy farmer, called Boaz. In time, they had a son, called Obed who became the grandfather of King David.

The Book of Ruth is one of the Ketuvim ("Writings") of the Hebrew *Bible* and forms part of the Christian Old Testament. Ruth's story teaches us about kindness and acceptance.

Find out more

Find out more about Ruth at:
www.chabad.org/theJewish
Woman/article_cdo/aid/2142/
jewish/The-Book-of-Ruth.htm

Solomon

Solomon was a king of ancient Israel and the son of King David (⇨p34). Famous for his wisdom, he also built the Holy Temple in Jerusalem.

About Solomon

During his long reign, Solomon organized several building projects, including the Holy Temple in Jerusalem. According to tradition, Solomon wrote three books of the *Bible* — the Book of Proverbs, Ecclesiastes, and the Song of Songs. He is also thought to have written several Psalms.

Find out more

Find out more about Solomon's reign at:
www.newadvent.org/
cathen/14135b.htm

Another great site is:
www.keyway.ca/htm2002/
solomon.htm

Timeline

Born in Jerusalem

Reigns as King of Israel

c. 1000 BC	c. 967	c. 967–928 BC

King David dies

Guru Angad Dev

Guru Angad Dev was the second **Sikh Guru**. He introduced the Gurmukhi script in which the Sikh language Punjabi is written.

About Guru Angad

Guru Angad Dev was brought up as a Hindu but became a follower of Guru Nanak. Guru Nanak named him as his successor rather than one of his sons. Guru Angad helped to make the Sikh religion stronger.

Find out more

Find out more about Guru Angad Dev at:
www.sikh-history.com/sikhhist/gurus/nanak2.html

Timeline

Born in Muktsar, India

Becomes the second Sikh Guru

1504　　　**1520**　　　**1539**　　　**1552**

Marries Mata Khivi

Dies in Amritsar, India

Guru Arjan

Guru Arjan was the fifth Sikh Guru. He compiled the **Guru Granth Sahib** (right) – the Sikhs' sacred text.

About Guru Arjan

Guru Arjan organized the building of the **Harimandir** ("Golden Temple") in Amritsar. He also compiled the *Guru Granth Sahib* from the writings of previous the Gurus, as well as poems by Hindu and Muslim holy men.

Find out more

Find out more about Guru Arjan at:
www.sikhs.org/guru5.htm

Timeline

Born in Goindval, India

Compiles the *Guru Granth Sahib*

1563　　　**1581**　　　c. **1604**　　　**1606**

Becomes the fifth Sikh Guru

Dies in Lahore, in modern-day Pakistan

Guru Gobind Singh

Guru Gobind Singh was the tenth Sikh Guru. He was a great scholar and brave soldier, who named the *Guru Granth Sahib* as his successor.

What he said

66 O Lord God, You are without any form, Class or symbol. None can describe your form, Features or shape. 99

(The Jap Sahib prayer)

How did he die?

Guru Gobind Singh died after being wounded by **assassins**.

Find out more

Find out more about Guru Gobind Singh at: www.sikhs.org/guru10.htm

The BBC website has more information about Guru Gobind Singh: www.bbc.co.uk/religion/religions/ sikhism/people/gobindsingh.shtml

Life of Guru Gobind Singh

Gobind Singh was born in Patna, India. He grew up to be a skilled horseman and warrior. When his family moved to Anandpur, he studied languages and composed many verses and poems. He became Guru at the age of nine, when his father was beheaded by the **Mughal** emperor, Aurangzeb.

Timeline

Born in Patna, India		Establishes the Khalsa		Meets with Emperor Bahadur Shah	
1666	**1675**	**1699**	**1705**	**1707**	**1708**
	Becomes the tenth Sikh Guru		Survives the siege of Anandpur		Dies in Nander, India

Place in religion

One of Guru Gobind Singh's greatest contributions to the Sikh religion was to establish the **Khalsa**. In 1699, Guru Gobind Singh chose five Sikhs to be the first members of the Khalsa. They were called the Panj Pyare, or "Pure Ones".

Guru Gobind Singh was the last human Guru. Before he died, he took five coins and a coconut, the symbols of the Guruship, and placed them in front the *Guru Granth Sahib*. He told his followers that the *Guru Granth Sahib* would be their Guru after his death.

Guru Hargobind

Guru Hargobind was the sixth Sikh Guru. He taught Sikhs to defend their faith against the Mughal rulers of India.

Life of Guru Hargobind

Hargobind became Guru when his father, Guru Arjan (⇨p41) was killed by the Mughal emperor, Jahangir. Guru Hargobind realized that the Sikhs needed to fight to defend their faith. He raised an army and built a fortress. Guru Hargobind wore two swords to symbolize spiritual and worldly power. He also organized the building of the Akal Takhat ("Immortal Throne") in Amritsar (shown top right). This remains the centre for Sikh religious authority.

What he said

66 He will have means not only to overcome his own hunger, but also to satisfy the hunger of many others. 99

(Blessing by Guru Hargobind)

Timeline

Born in Amritsar, India

Fights a series of battles against Mughals

Dies in Kiratpur, India

| 1595 | 1606 | 1628-34 | 1634 | 1644 |

Becomes the sixth Sikh Guru

Moves to Kiratpur in the Punjab

Find out more

Find out more about Guru Hargobind at: www.sikh-history.com/ sikhhist/gurus/nanak6.html

This website has more information about the life of Guru Hargobind: www.sikhs.org/guru6.htm

Find out more about the festival of Diwali at the BBC website: www.bbc.co.uk/religion/ religions/hinduism/holydays/diwali.shtml

Place in religion

When the Emperor Jahangir's fell ill, he sent Guru Hargobind to a fort to pray for him. The fort was also a prison that held 52 Hindu princes. When the emperor recovered, he ordered the Guru to be released. Guru Hargobind would not leave without the princes. The emperor agreed that any princes that could hold on to the Guru's cloak would be freed. So Guru Hargobind made a cloak with 52 tassels and led all the princes to freedom. Sikhs remember this story at the festival of Diwali.

How did he die?

Guru Hargobind died peacefully in Kiratpur at the age of 49.

Guru Nanak

Guru Nanak was the first Guru of the Sikh religion. He travelled widely, teaching tolerance and equality for everyone.

What he said

66 There is only one God and God is the only truth. God the creator is without fear, without hate and immortal. God is beyond death. God is understood through God's grace. 99

(Mool Mantar prayer)

Did you know?

The *Guru Granth Sahib* includes 974 of Guru Nanak's hymns.

Find out more

Find out more about Guru Nanak and his teachings at: http://atschool.eduweb.co.uk/carolrb/sikhism/nanak.html

The BBC website has more information about Guru Nanak: www.bbc.co.uk/schools/religion/sikhism/gurunanak.shtml

Another great page on the BBC website: www.bbc.co.uk/schools/religion/sikhism/

Life of Guru Nanak

Nanak was born into a Hindu family and became interested in religion from an early age. When he was about 30 years old, Nanak went missing for several days. He returned and told people that God had called him. From then on, he gave up his job and belongings. He devoted his life to teaching people about God.

Timeline

Born in Talwandi, in modern-day Pakistan

1469

1499

Becomes the first Sikh Guru

Marries Sulakhani

1481

1539

Dies in Kartapur, India

Place in religion

Guru Nanak is the founder of Sikhism. Sikhs believe that there is one God who considers everyone to be equal. Sikhs can grow closer to God by caring for others, working hard, and remembering God in everything they do. Guru Nanak often used verses to explain his teachings. These were set to music by his travelling companion, Mardana.

Every year, in October or November, Sikhs celebrate Guru Nanak's birthday. It is the most important time in the Sikh calendar. There is a reading of the *Guru Granth Sahib*, worship in the temple, and street processions.

Guru Ram Das

Guru Ram Das was the fourth Sikh Guru. He founded the holy city of Amritsar in India (shown right).

About Guru Ram Das

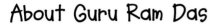

Guru Ram Das succeeded Guru Amar Das and married his Guru's daughter. Guru Ram Das is best remember for founding the holy city of Amritsar. He also wrote the four verses of the Lavan – the Sikh wedding hymn.

Find out more

Find out more about Guru Ram Das at: www.sikh-history.com/ sikhhist/gurus/nanak4.html

Timeline

1534	1574	1577	1581
Born in Lahore, in modern-day Pakistan	Becomes the fourth Sikh Guru	Begins work on Amritsar, India	Dies in Amritsar

Guru Tegh Bahadur

Guru Tegh Bahadur was the ninth Sikh Guru. He composed many hymns in the *Guru Granth Sahib*.

About Guru Tegh Bahadur

Guru Tegh Bahadur founded the city of Anandpur (shown right). He travelled widely, teaching people about the Sikh faith. Guru Tegh Bahadur was beheaded by the Mughal emperor, Aurangzeb, because he refused to give up his Sikh faith.

Find out more

Find out more about Guru Tegh Bahadur at: www.sikh-history.com/ sikhhist/gurus/nanak9.html

Timeline

1621	1633	1665	1675
Born in Amritsar, India	Marries Gujari	Becomes the ninth Sikh Guru	Mughal emperor executes him

Glossary

Arabic The language of the Arabs, in which the *Qur'an* (the holy book of Islam) is written.

assassin Person who murders an important figure.

avatar In Hindu belief, the body a god takes in order to visit the Earth.

baptized A ceremony which marks a person's new life as a Christian.

Bible The Christian holy book.

bishop A very senior priest or minister in the Christian Church.

Buddhist A follower of the Buddha's teachings; to do with Buddhism.

Christian A follower of Jesus Christ; to do with Christianity.

civil war A war between two areas in the same country.

crucified Being killed by being nailed to a cross and left to die.

crusades Wars fought between the Christians and Muslims in the 11th and 13th centuries.

Disciples Followers of a religious leader or teacher.

enlightenment The experience of realizing the truth.

Guru One of the ten Sikhs who taught Sikhism between 1499 and 1708.

Guru Granth Sahib The holy book of the Sikhs.

Hajj The pilgrimage to Makkah which all Muslims try to make at least once in their lives.

Harimandir The Sikhs' holiest building, in Amritsar, India. It is also known as the "Golden Temple".

Hebrew The language of Israel and the Jewish people.

hermit A person, often a religious person, who lives alone in an isolated place.

incarnation The body or form a deity or religious figure takes to visit the Earth.

invincible Very strong; unlikely to be beaten or defeated.

Islam A religion which began in Arabia (Saudi Arabia) about 1,400 years ago.

Jewish Someone or something that is part of the Jewish faith, Judaism.

Judaism A religion which began in the Middle East more than 4,000 years ago.

Ka'bah A cube-shaped building in Makkah. Muslims turn to face the Ka'bah when they pray.

Khalsa The Sikh community begun by Guru Gobind Singh in 1699.

mantra A short prayer that may be chanted over and over again.

meditating Thinking deeply or concentrating on just one thought to achieve a feeling of calm.

missionary A person who works to convert others to their faith.

monk A man who has devoted himself to his religion, and given up his home and possessions.

Mughal The Muslim rulers of India from the 16th and 18th centuries.

Muslim A follower of the religion of Islam; to do with Islam.

patron saint A very holy person particularly linked to a place or activity.

persecuted When people are treated badly, and even killed, because of their religion.

Pharaoh The title given to the king in ancient Egypt.

pilgrim A person who travels to a holy place that is important in their religion.

Pope The head of the Roman Catholic Church (in Christianity).

psalms In the Christian and Jewish holy book, psalms are songs of praise to God.

reincarnation To be born again in another body.

Sanskrit Ancient Indian language.

Sikh A follower of the religion of Sikhism; to do with Sikhism.

synagogue A place where Jews go to worship and learn about their religion.

Index